# God Made Them, And He Does Not Make Junk

## Honoring God's Creativity in Others

Cindy H. Carr, D.Min., MACL

This book is published by **CHC Connect**.

All views and opinions expressed in this work are those of the author. Any errors or omissions are unintentional.

Printed in the United States of America
First Edition, 2025

**ISBN: 978-1-971192-04-8**

For permissions or inquiries, contact:
**Cindy H. Carr**
cindyhcarr@outlook.com
www.cindyhcarr.com

# About This Series

In a world that often questions our worth, **The Made by God Series** gently brings us back to a simple, powerful truth: God created each of us with intention, care, and purpose.

This series leads readers on a journey—from understanding who you are in God's eyes, to recognizing His unique design in others, to living together in authentic, life-giving community. With warmth and clarity you see that every person bears God's imprint, and that we are meant to live that truth out together.

Because God made you, God made them, and together, God made us—and He does not make junk.

- **Book 1**
  *God Made You, And He Does Not Make Junk: Discovering the You That God Had in Mind*
- **Book 2**
  *God Made Them, And He Does Not Make Junk: Honoring God's Creativity in Others*
- **Book 3**
  *God Made Us, And He Does Not Make Junk: Stronger Together*

**Visit www.cindyhcarr.com to view the full catalog.**

# Acknowledgment

This acknowledgment is for my husband, Dubby.

We married on June 19, 1982, and it didn't take long to discover we were very different—different rhythms, different instincts, different lenses. And if I'm honest, there were seasons when our differences felt like obstacles instead of gifts. But so much of what lives inside this book was born in those real-life moments: learning, stretching, failing, trying again, and slowly discovering the kindness of God hidden inside "not like me."

Dubby, I am grateful for the journey of learning how God created you. I'm grateful for the steady ways you love, the ways you see what I miss, and the ways your design has strengthened our home—even when I didn't recognize it.

I will never forget the day I came to God with a list of complaints—convinced I was bringing Him important information. And instead of answering the way I expected, I heard the Lord say, **"I am pleased with your husband."** Of course, that was not what I wanted to hear in that moment. It felt like God gently took every accusation out of my hands and replaced it with honor.

Dubby, thank you for building a life with me. Thank you for staying, for growing, for forgiving, and for letting God shape us into a stronger "us." This book carries many lessons I learned because I married you. And I can say with joy, after all these years: I'm still learning—and I'm still grateful.

# Introduction

God didn't create you to live on a private island with Him alone. It was God's idea to put us in families, workplaces, friendships, neighborhoods, and communities.

And that's where the joy—and the challenge—shows up.

Because once you begin to see your own design clearly, you start noticing something else: the people around you were designed too. And sometimes their wiring feels like it clashes with yours.

Maybe you're a list person and they're spontaneous. Maybe you recharge alone and they recharge with people. Maybe you're detail-first and they're big-picture. Maybe you're gentle and they're direct. Maybe you're a peacemaker and they're a challenger.

And if we're not careful, we can start interpreting difference as a negative thing.

But what if this is God's creativity on display? What if it's design?

This book is built on a simple conviction: God created them… and He does not make junk.

That means the person who frustrates you may be carrying a gift you need. The person you don't understand may be protecting something good. And the person whose lens is opposite yours may be part of how God stretches you into maturity.

Scripture supports this. From the beginning, God looked at His creation and called it "very good" (Genesis 1:31, NIV). And when Paul talks about people working together, he describes "many parts" making "one body" (Romans 12:4–5, NIV). Different parts. One purpose.

So this is not a book about labeling people. It's a book about learning to recognize God's creativity in others—and then learning how to walk in love with people who are not wired like you.

We're going to use Scripture as our anchor and bring in a few helpful translation lenses—things like DISC, Myers-Briggs[2], and other tools—not as identity, not as destiny, and definitely not as a crutch. Just as vocabulary. Because sometimes you don't need a new belief; you need new words for what you're already experiencing.

We'll keep it practical. We'll keep it hopeful. And we'll keep it honest—because the goal isn't to pretend relationships are easy. The goal is to learn the skills that make them healthier.

My posture in writing is the same posture I've carried for years when I talk to people: I speak to you like you already love God. Not because your story is perfect, but because God stamped His image on every human life. And when you taste even a little of His love, it becomes contagious. When we live intentionally connected to the God who created us, we grow into our truest selves-and we learn to see the beauty of His craftmanship in the people around us.

So here's what I'm praying as you read: that you will feel hopeful and energized, that you will gain language for what you've struggled to explain, and that you will discover the joy God had when He made the people around you—especially the ones most unlike you.

Because when we learn to honor design—ours and theirs—we start building what God intended all along: us.

# Table of Contents

# How to Use This Book

This book is written like a coaching conversation—warm, practical, and meant to be lived, not just read.

Read it your way

You can read straight through from Chapter 1 to the end, and you'll feel the progression:

• foundation (very good)

• seeing people well

• unity without forced agreement

• translation lenses

• real-life application (family, work, conflict, boundaries, forgiveness)

• putting it all together

But if you're in a specific season—parenting tension, workplace strain, friendship friction—you can also jump to the chapter you need most.

Use the 'Try this sentence' prompts

Most chapters include a "Try this sentence." That's intentional.

You don't need more theory. You need words you can use in real time—in the kitchen, on the phone, in the meeting, or in the car when you're replaying a conversation.

Pick one sentence and practice it this week. That's enough. (I told you—no heavy homework!)

Treat reflection as optional

Each chapter includes a short reflection section. If you love journaling, it's for you. If you don't, you're free to skip it without guilt.

Some people process by writing. Others process by walking, praying, or talking it out. God is not grading your reflection pages.

Let Scripture stay woven and lightweight

You'll notice Scripture is often quoted in short phrases inside sentences. That's on purpose—so the book reads smoothly and converts cleanly for eBook.

I primarily use NIV, and occasionally NLT or another translation when the wording fits the moment. When we finalize the manuscript, we'll note translation choices where needed.

Hold tools in the right place

When we mention tools like DISC or Myers-Briggs, remember the rule:

**Tools are vocabulary, not verdicts.**

A tool can help you translate patterns. Only God transforms hearts. So don't use tools to label people or excuse yourself. Use them to grow in honor, humility, and love. Keep the big goal in front of you

This is not about becoming a personality expert. It's about becoming the kind of person who can build healthy relationships—who can see the gift in others, speak with honor, repair quickly, hold boundaries cleanly, and stay united even when you don't agree.

If you walk away from this book with more curiosity, more compassion, and even one new sentence that changes your relationships—then we're doing exactly what I hoped.

A simple rhythm (if you want one)

Here's a simple way to move through the book without pressure:

1) Read one chapter.

2) Pick one "Try this sentence."

3) Use it once this week.

4) If you mess it up, repair quickly. (That counts as progress.)

Small steps. Clean love. Real growth.

# Chapter 1: Very Good — God's Joyful Design for People

Before we talk about how to understand people, we have to start where God started: with delight.

If you read Book 1, God Made You and He Does Not Make Junk, you know what it feels like when the lights come on—when you realize your design isn't random, your story isn't wasted, and God wasn't improvising when He made you. There's a holy kind of excitement that rises up when you can finally say, "Oh… this is how God wired me."

I want to carry that same excitement into this book. Because the truth is, the God who delighted in designing you also delighted in designing the people around you. And once you start seeing others through that lens, everything changes. You stop bracing for differences—and you start getting curious about them.

Sometimes we begin the "learning to love people" journey from the wrong starting line. We begin with frustration— "Why are they like that?"—or fear— "What if I'm misunderstood?"—or exhaustion— "I don't have the capacity for one more personality."

But Genesis doesn't begin with frustration. It begins with creative joy. God speaks, God forms, God breathes—and then He looks at what He has made and calls it good. And when He creates humanity—men and women made in His image—Scripture says He looked at it all and called it "very good" (Genesis 1:31, NIV).

Not "good enough." Not "acceptable." Not "fine." Very good.

That one phrase is the foundation of this entire book, because it changes what we believe about people before we ever try to relate to them. If God calls His creation very good, then people are not problems to solve. They are workmanship to honor.

And yes—people can be wounded. People can be immature. People can be selfish. But even there, under the mess, God's intention still matters. His design still matters. Because God didn't create junk.

## God Didn't Create Sameness—He Created Variety

We live in a world that often rewards sameness. Sameness feels efficient. Predictable. Easier to manage. If everyone thinks like me, moves like me, processes like me, communicates like me—then life feels smoother.

But the Bible doesn't present sameness as the goal. It presents love as the goal. And love requires difference—because love is the skill of honoring someone who is not you.

You can see God's love for variety everywhere. Look at creation itself: oceans and deserts, mountains and plains, eagles and ants, towering trees and tiny seeds. God is not a minimalistic creator. He is an artist.

So why would we assume He became boring when He created people?

In real life, variety shows up in everyday ways:

• Some people are list people. Some people are spontaneous.

• Some people recharge around people. Some people recharge in quiet.

• Some people lead with big-picture vision. Some people lead with careful detail.

• Some people talk to think. Some people think before they talk.

• Some people feel love through words. Others feel love through actions.

None of those differences are moral failures. They are unique design.

And if we don't understand that, we will do what humans naturally do: we will judge other people by our preference and call it wisdom.

### The Hidden Default: We Prefer Our Own Wiring

Here's a truth most of us don't like admitting—until God makes it undeniable:

**We tend to prefer our own wiring.**

Even when we're insecure. Even when we're unsure of ourselves. It's wild how quickly we assume our way is the "normal" way.

So a structured person can look at a flexible person and think, "They're irresponsible." And a flexible person can look at a structured person and think, "They're controlling."

A direct person can look at a gentle person and think, "They're weak." A gentle person can look at a direct person and think, "They're harsh."

A cautious person can look at a risk-taker and think, "They're reckless." A risk-taker can look at a cautious person and think, "They're negative."

And here's the problem: when we move into judgment, we stop being curious. And when curiosity dies, relationships shrink.

This is why the starting line matters. If we start from "very good," we approach people with honor. Honor doesn't mean agreement. Honor means we begin with the assumption that God's design is present—even if it's covered in stress or immaturity.

### A Different Question

So the question changes. Instead of…

"Why are they like that?"

We learn to ask…

"What did God place in them on purpose?"

That question doesn't make you naïve. It makes you wise.

Because when you can name what someone is trying to protect, you stop making them the enemy. You start seeing their contribution.

### The Image of God Is Revealed in 'Us,' Not Just 'Me'

Here is one of the big revelations God wants to give you through this book:

**Every person is needed to reflect God's image more fully.**

Not because every person is always right. Not because every opinion is equal. But because God's creativity is so wide that one person cannot carry the full reflection of His nature alone.

That's why Scripture talks about the body—many parts, one body. Different functions, one purpose. A hand is not less than an eye. An ear is not less than a foot. We need each other.

And this is where the joy comes back: when you realize that other people's differences aren't interruptions. They are often invitations.

An invitation to grow. An invitation to broaden your love. An invitation to see God from another angle.

**How 'Very Good' Changes Real Life**

Let's make this practical. If "very good" is true, here are a few changes it produces in everyday relationships:

**1) It changes how you interpret irritation**

Irritation is often a signal—not that someone is bad—but that a difference is present. Sometimes the irritation is exposing your unhealed places. Sometimes it's exposing a lack of skill. And sometimes it's simply exposing a preference you've been calling "right."

When you feel irritation rise, instead of letting it become accusation, use it as a cue to translate.

### 2) It changes how you interpret slowness

Some people are quick processors. Some people are slow processors. Quick can be a gift. Slow can be a gift. Quick often protects momentum. Slow often protects quality and depth.

When you start from "very good," you stop shaming slowness and you stop mocking speed. You start building a rhythm that includes both.

### 3) It changes how you interpret disagreement

Disagreement is not always disunity. Sometimes disagreement is simply two people protecting two different good things.

In later chapters we'll talk more about unity not always being agreement, but here's the seed of it: you can respect someone without matching them.

### Try this sentence

"Before I react, let me remember: God called this person 'very good.'"

That sentence doesn't mean you ignore problems. It means you approach problems without contempt.

### A Small Practice That Changes Everything: Name the Good First

If you want a simple practice that will shift your relationships immediately, it's this:

**Name the good first.**

You'd be amazed how many conflicts dissolve when people feel seen for their intention.

It can sound like:

- "I can see you care about this."

- "I can see you're trying to protect something important."

- "I can see you're carrying a lot."

- "Thank you for caring enough to speak up."

Then—once you've named the good—you can address the tension with a totally different tone. Truth with dignity. Correction without humiliation. Boundaries without bitterness.

**Optional reflection**

Where do you most often assume "different" means "difficult"? Ask God to give you one specific person to practice 'very good' with this week. Not by approving everything they do, but by honoring the workmanship God placed in them.

**Prayer**

Father, thank You for the joy of Your design. You are not a creator of junk. Open my eyes to see people the way You see them—very good, purposeful, loved. Deliver me from quick judgment and hidden contempt. Teach me to honor differences, translate what I don't understand, and build unity with love. In Jesus' name, amen.

**Bridge to Chapter 2:** Now that we've anchored our starting line—"very good"—we can learn the next skill: seeing people the way God sees them in real time.

# Chapter 2: Seeing People the Way God Sees Them

If Chapter 1 gave us our starting line—"very good"—then Chapter 2 gives us the next skill: learning to see people that way in real time.

Because it's one thing to agree with Genesis in theory. It's another thing to hold on to "very good" when someone's tone is sharp, when their timing is terrible, when their personality clashes with yours, or when their story is messy.

Seeing people the way God sees them is the backbone of learning how to understand them. It's also the backbone of learning how to work with them.

And Scripture gives us a scene that feels surprisingly modern—Jesus, tired and thirsty, sitting beside a well, and one conversation changing everything (John 4, NIV).

## Jesus at the Well: A Masterclass in Seeing People Well

John tells us Jesus was traveling and stopped at a well around noon. That detail matters. Noon was the hottest part of the day. Most women would have come to draw water in the cooler hours—morning or evening.

So when a woman shows up alone at noon, you can hear the unspoken story: she's not there because it's convenient. She's there because it's quiet. She's there because fewer eyes will be watching.

This is what people do when they've been judged long enough. They manage exposure. They choose low-visibility moments. They arrange their life so they don't have to face the same look… again.

Then Jesus does something that would have been socially unexpected—He talks to her. He doesn't start with a lecture. He starts with a simple request: "Will you give me a drink?" (John 4:7, NIV).

It's a small sentence, but it's full of dignity. He doesn't approach her like she's a case study. He approaches her like she's a person.

**Notice what Jesus doesn't do**

- He doesn't lead with her reputation.
- He doesn't act shocked by her life.
- He doesn't treat her as an interruption.
- He doesn't use truth as a weapon.

Jesus sees her whole. He sees her story, her thirst, her questions, her longing, her dignity—and He still offers her living water.

If you want a simple definition of what it means to see people the way God sees them, it's this:

**You look past the label and you look for the person.**

That doesn't mean we ignore truth. Jesus didn't ignore truth. But He placed truth inside honor—so it could be received.

### The Two Places We Usually Get Stuck

Most of us don't struggle to see people the way God sees them when it's easy. We struggle when it costs us something.

#### 1) We get stuck on behavior

Behavior is the surface. Behavior is what you can see. It's the tone, the timing, the decision, the comment, the reaction.

But behavior is rarely the whole story. Underneath behavior is usually something being protected.

Some people protect control because they've lived through chaos. Some people protect independence because they've been let down. Some people protect humor because they're afraid of pain. Some people protect anger because it feels safer than vulnerability.

When you learn to look underneath the behavior, your compassion grows—without becoming naïve.

**2) We get stuck on our own reaction**

Sometimes the biggest barrier to seeing people well is not what they're doing. It's what their behavior triggers in us.

Someone's directness triggers your fear of being controlled. Someone's silence triggers your fear of being abandoned. Someone's intensity triggers your fear of conflict. Someone's mess triggers your fear of being judged.

This is why God often uses relationships as formation. He isn't just revealing what's in them. He's revealing what's in us.

**A Coaching Shift: From Assumption to Curiosity**

If you want to live this chapter, you don't need a theology degree. You need one simple shift: replace assumption with curiosity.

Assumption sounds like: "They're doing this to me." Curiosity sounds like: "Help me understand your lens."

Assumption escalates. Curiosity de-escalates.

Curiosity doesn't mean you agree. Curiosity means you're willing to learn before you label.

**Try this sentence**

"Help me understand your lens—what matters most to you about this?"

That sentence is one of the most powerful relationship tools you will ever use. It communicates respect. It slows the moment down. It invites the person out of defense.

### The 'Protect' Question: The Fastest Way to Understand People

When someone's response doesn't make sense, ask this question—either out loud or in your own heart:

**What might they be trying to protect?**

In Chapter 1, we said differences are often coverage. This question helps you discover what kind of coverage you're looking at.

Here are a few common "protect" categories:

- Quality and accuracy
- Stability and peace
- Connection and belonging
- Safety and integrity
- Respect and dignity

When you can name what someone is trying to protect, you stop making them the enemy.

### Seeing People Well Doesn't Mean You Lose Yourself

A common fear is: "If I try to understand people, I'll get walked on."

Understanding is not surrender. Seeing people well doesn't require you to abandon boundaries. It requires you to approach boundaries without contempt.

Even Jesus, who saw people perfectly, didn't say yes to every demand. He stayed faithful to the Father's assignment.

So here is the balanced truth: you can honor someone and still say no. You can see someone and still set a limit. You can be compassionate and still be clear.

### A Quick Practice: Name the Good, Then the Need

If you want to apply Jesus' well-conversation in everyday life, here's a simple practice:

**Step 1: Name the good you see**

"I can see you care about this."

"I can tell this matters to you."

"I appreciate your effort."

**Step 2: Name what you need or what needs to change**

"And I need us to slow down and talk respectfully."

"And I need clarity on what we're deciding."

"And I need a boundary around how we speak to each other."

This is truth with dignity. This is seeing people well without shrinking yourself.

**A Word for the Person Who Feels 'Othered'-like you don't belong**

If you're the person who often feels misunderstood, overlooked, judged, or "othered,"-treated like an outsider- hear this: Jesus sees you. Fully. Kindly. Clearly.

The woman at the well had plenty of reasons to believe she would be dismissed. But Jesus engaged her in one of the longest recorded conversations He has with any individual in the Gospels.

That's not accidental. That's what God's love looks like when it shows up in real life.

**Memorable moment**

**People don't change most from being corrected. People change most from being seen.**

**Optional reflection**

Think of one relationship where you feel stuck.
1) Where are you assuming motive?
2) What might the other person be trying to protect?
3) What is one question you could ask that would shift the conversation from heat to understanding?

**Prayer**

Jesus, thank You for the way You see people—truthful and kind, clear and compassionate. Teach me to see people the way You do. Deliver me from quick labels and hidden contempt. Give me curiosity, honor, and wisdom. Help me speak truth with dignity and hold boundaries with love. In Your name, amen.

**Bridge to Chapter 3**: Once we learn to see people well, the next step is learning to stay united even when we don't agree—because unity is not always agreement.

# Chapter 3: Unity Is Not Always Agreement

By now we've set our starting line: what God made is "very good." And we've begun practicing the skill of seeing people the way God sees them—looking past labels, asking better questions, and learning to translate differences.

Now comes a truth that will protect your relationships more than almost anything else:

**Unity is not always agreement.**

If you can settle that in your heart, you will stop trying to force people to match you in order to stay connected to you. And you will stop assuming disagreement automatically means disloyalty, division, or disrespect.

We live in a world that often tells us we have two options: either agree or separate. But Scripture gives us a third option: stay united while you navigate difference with love, humility, and wisdom.

## The Problem Behind So Many Problems: We Confuse Agreement with Safety

Many of us learned—without anyone ever saying it out loud—that agreement equals safety. If we all see it the same way, then no one gets hurt. No one gets rejected. No one gets labeled.

But agreement is not the same thing as unity. Agreement is matching conclusions. Unity is protecting relationship and shared purpose.

In real life, people can agree and still have no unity. They can sit at the same table and be full of contempt. And people can disagree and still have deep unity—because their hearts are committed to love.

This is why the phrase "unity is not always agreement" is not a cute quote. It's a lifeline.

### The Early Church Didn't Avoid Disagreement—They Learned How to Navigate It

One of the most honest chapters in the New Testament is Acts 15. The early church faced a serious disagreement: what should be required of Gentile believers? It wasn't a minor preference. It was a question that touched identity, belonging, tradition, and theology.

If you want to see a model for unity without forced agreement, Acts 15 is a masterclass.

**Notice what they did:**

• They named the issue openly.

• They listened to one another.

• They considered what God was doing—not just what people preferred.

• They protected the mission.

• They chose a path that kept the door open for people to belong and grow.

They didn't pretend the tension wasn't real. They didn't silence people. They did the spiritual work of listening, discerning, and choosing love.

And here is a key coaching point: unity is not passive. Unity is not avoiding hard conversations. Unity is an active commitment to stay connected while we work through difference with honor.

## A Modern Example: A Mentor Friendship That Chose Respect Over the Weeds

Some of the richest friendships in my life have been the ones that didn't require sameness. They required respect.

One of my spiritual mentors and I came from very different theological lenses. One of us came from a worldview that emphasized the sovereignty of God—

everything that takes place is in God's hands. The other of us came from more of an Arminian lens—human choice carries real weight, and sometimes God walks alongside us as we experience the ramifications of our decisions; yet God is always for us, and He never wastes a crisis in drawing us closer and forming character.

Those are huge differences. They shape how you interpret suffering, timing, unanswered prayer, even how you see God's involvement in everyday life.

But those differences didn't reduce our friendship. They deepened it.

We were able to have the richest, most meaningful conversations. And sometimes we would laugh and say, "Okay—here's my terminology. You just translate that into however you need to understand it."

That sentence created a culture of peace between us. It acknowledged something mature: we didn't have to win each other over to keep loving each other well.

**Respect is often the bridge between difference and unity.**

Because if you can see God in someone—even if their theology is totally different than yours—it's beautiful. It's a gift.

## Unity Requires a Shared 'Main Thing'

Unity is not built on pretending differences don't exist. Unity is built on deciding what matters most.

In Christian language, that's often described as "keeping the main thing the main thing." But this principle also works for the broad audience we're speaking to—because every healthy relationship has to decide what it's actually built on.

Families are built on more than preferences. Friendships are built on more than matching opinions. Work teams are built on more than identical personalities. They're built on shared values, shared purpose, and shared respect.

And when you can't find any shared main thing—when there is no mutual respect, no mutual value, no mutual willingness to honor—that's information. And wise people use information to move forward with clarity and peace.

## The Translation Skill: 'Tell Me What You Mean'

One of the easiest ways to protect unity is to realize that we can use the same words but mean different things.

That was the gift in my mentor friendship. We didn't always share terminology, but we shared respect. So instead of fighting over language, we translated.

**Translation is not compromise. Translation is honor.**

Translation asks questions like:

- "When you say that, what do you mean?"
- "What are you trying to protect?"
- "What are you afraid might happen if we do it the other way?"
- "What matters most to you about this?"

When you translate, you stop assuming the worst. And when you stop assuming the worst, your heart stays softer.

## What Unity Is Not

Unity is not agreement, but unity is also not enabling.

Unity does not mean:

- you tolerate contempt.
- you stay in conversations where you are being demeaned.
- you ignore repeated harmful behavior.
- you abandon your convictions to keep the peace.
- you keep forcing a fit that consistently produces harm.

Unity is not pretending. Unity is honest love.

Sometimes unity looks like staying at the table and talking it through. Sometimes unity looks like taking a break and coming back later. And sometimes unity looks like changing lanes so that everyone can be healthier.

We'll talk more about that later, because even the disciples sometimes worked separately. There is wisdom in recognizing that not every environment is a good fit for your healthiest wiring. Separation is not always failure. Sometimes it is stewardship.

**Try this sentence**

"I can honor your love for God, even if we see this differently."

If the person you're speaking with does not share your faith language, you can translate it this way:

"I can respect you, even if we don't agree."

### Three Coaching Rules for Unity Without Agreement

#### 1) Start with honor, not heat

Honor doesn't mean you agree. Honor means you acknowledge dignity. It changes the air in the room.

**2) Name what you share**

Before you go deep into where you differ, name what you share—values, goals, relationship, purpose.

**3) Decide what kind of conversation this is**

Not every disagreement needs a debate. Some disagreements need a decision. Some need a boundary. Some need a pause. Some are simply two lenses protecting two different good things.

**Memorable moment**

**You don't have to agree with someone to honor the image of God in them.**

**Optional reflection**

Think of one relationship where disagreement has created distance.
1) What is the shared 'main thing' you can name?
2) What translation question could you ask instead of making an assumption?
3) What would honor look like in one sentence?

**Prayer**

Father, teach me to protect unity without demanding sameness. Give me humility to listen, courage to speak with kindness, and wisdom to know when to stay, when to pause, and when to change lanes. Help me honor Your image in people even when we don't see things the same way. In Jesus' name, amen.

**Bridge to Chapter 4**: Once unity is protected, we can start to appreciate how different strengths work together—and how quickly strengths can drift into shadows under pressure.

# Chapter 4: Two Sisters, Two Lenses — Learning to Honor Different Strengths

If Chapter 3 taught us that unity is not always agreement, Chapter 4 teaches us something just as practical: difference is not automatically dysfunction.

Sometimes the tension you feel with another person isn't because either of you are "wrong." Sometimes it's because you're protecting different good things.

And one of the most relatable pictures of this is found in a simple home scene—two sisters, one moment, and one very honest emotional reaction.

It's the story of Mary and Martha (Luke 10:38–42, NIV).

**Mary and Martha: The Moment That Exposes the Tension**

Jesus and His disciples arrive in the village. Martha opens her home. Mary sits at Jesus' feet, listening. And Martha begins doing what hosts do: preparing, serving, managing, making sure people are cared for.

At first glance, it seems like a simple division of labor. But then you can almost feel the emotional temperature rise.

Luke says Martha was "distracted by all the preparations that had to be made" (Luke 10:40, NIV). That word distracted is important. It suggests her mind and heart were pulled in too many directions at once.

And then Martha does what many of us do under pressure—she assumes motive.

She comes to Jesus and says, in essence, "Don't you care that my sister has left me to do the work by myself? Tell her to help me." (Luke 10:40, NIV).

If you've ever snapped at someone, you can hear what's underneath her words. She doesn't feel supported. She doesn't feel seen. She doesn't feel partnered.

And because she doesn't feel supported, her frustration turns into accusation.

## What Each Sister Was Protecting

Here's why this story matters for us: both sisters were doing something good.

Martha was protecting hospitality. Care. Preparation. Stewardship. She was creating a space where Jesus and others could be served.

Mary was protecting presence. Listening. Connection. Spiritual attentiveness. She was receiving what Jesus was offering in that moment.

In other words: one sister was protecting the environment, and one sister was protecting the encounter.

If we translate that into modern life, you can see it everywhere:

- One person is focused on the task; the other is focused on the relationship.

- One person is focused on details; the other is focused on meaning.

- One person is focused on responsibility; the other is focused on being present.

- One person is focused on outcomes; the other is focused on process.

And when those differences aren't honored, they often turn into labels.

**How Good Strengths Drift into Shadows Under Pressure**

A big theme of this book is that strengths can drift into shadows when stress rises.

Martha's strength—responsibility—drifted into resentment. Mary's strength—presence—could drift into disengagement if she never participates in practical care.

This is where relationships become difficult: not because the strengths are bad, but because the pressure changes how they show up.

And the hidden danger is this: when we're under pressure, we tend to assume our own strength is the "right" way.

**Under stress, we turn preferences into moral judgments.**

A Martha can start to believe: "If you cared, you would help." A Mary can start to believe: "If you understood, you would slow down."

Neither one is entirely wrong. And neither one has the full picture alone.

**What Jesus Actually Does Here**

This story is often used to shame Martha, but I don't think that's Jesus' intent.

Jesus responds with tenderness: "Martha, Martha…" (Luke 10:41, NIV). In Scripture, repeating a name often communicates compassion, not annoyance.

Then He names what's happening inside her: "You are worried and upset about many things." (Luke 10:41, NIV).

Notice what He addresses: not her service, but her inner state.

In other words, the issue wasn't that she was serving. The issue was that she was serving from pressure instead of peace.

And then He affirms Mary's choice in that moment.

Jesus isn't saying preparation never matters. He's saying that in this moment, presence mattered most.

That's a key coaching point: sometimes two good things are present, but one is needed first.

**A Coaching Lens for Real Life: What Is Needed First?**

In families and friendships, one of the most common conflicts is when one person is trying to solve the problem and the other person is trying to feel connected.

One person wants a plan. The other wants empathy.

One person wants movement. The other wants understanding.

One person wants action. The other wants presence.

The Mary and Martha story teaches us to pause and ask: what is needed first?

Sometimes the answer is: we need to sit at the feet of Jesus first—before we run into motion.

And sometimes the answer is: we need to serve and carry responsibility—because love is practical.

The best relationships learn to do both.

**Try this sentence**

"I can see what you're protecting. Help me know what you need first—presence or a plan?"

That sentence is powerful because it does two things at once: it honors the person and it creates clarity.

### A Simple Practice: Name the Good Before You Name the Gap

If you want to stop Mary/Martha conflict in your real life, here is one simple practice:

**Step 1: Name the good you see**

"Thank you for carrying this."

"I see how much you care."

"I appreciate the way you're showing up."

**Step 2: Name the gap without accusation**

"And I need us to do this together."

"And I need a few minutes of presence before we jump into tasks."

"And I need a plan so I don't feel overwhelmed."

When you name the good first, you protect the relationship while addressing what needs to change.

## When You're the Martha: How to Come Back to Peace

If you tend to be more like Martha—responsible, prepared, quick to carry—here is a gentle truth: your gift is beautiful. The world needs it.

But your gift becomes heavy when you carry it alone and expect others to think like you.

Instead of letting resentment build, practice asking clearly for help before you explode.

**Try this sentence**

"I'm feeling overloaded. Could you help me with two specific things?"

Specific is kind. Specific keeps your request from becoming a complaint.

### When You're the Mary: How to Stay Present and Still Participate

If you tend to be more like Mary—present, reflective, relational—your gift is also beautiful. The world needs people who know how to slow down and listen.

But your gift can become confusing to others if they feel like you never show up practically.

Sometimes love looks like saying, "I'm here with you," and sometimes it looks like grabbing a plate and helping with the dishes.

**Try this sentence**

"I want to be fully present—and I also want to help. What's one practical thing I can do right now?"

**Memorable moment**

**Your difference is not a threat. It's often your contribution.**

**Optional reflection**

In your closest relationships, do you lean more Mary or Martha?

1) What strength is God contributing through you?
2) What shadow shows up when you're stressed?
3) What would it look like to honor the other person's contribution this week—in one sentence?

**Prayer**

Father, thank You for the beauty of Your design. Teach me to honor different strengths without labeling or comparison. Help me recognize when I'm serving from pressure instead of peace, and when I'm present without participating in love's practical needs. Make me wise enough to ask what's needed first. Teach me to build relationships where both presence and preparation can thrive. In Jesus' name, amen.

**Bridge to Chapter 5**: Once we learn to honor different strengths, we can learn the next skill—recognizing when strengths drift into shadows under pressure, and how to repair quickly.

# Chapter 5: Strength and Shadow — What Pressure Reveals (and How to Repair Quickly)

By now, we've established two foundational truths: God's design is "very good," and difference is often contribution.

But there's a reality we also have to name if we want this book to be practical: even good design can look messy when pressure is high.

People don't always show you their best self when they're tired, afraid, overwhelmed, or wounded. Sometimes they show you their stressed self. And if you don't recognize that, you can misread someone's wiring as someone's character.

Here's the coaching truth that saves relationships:

**Under pressure, strengths can drift into shadows.**

That doesn't mean the strength is bad. It means the strength is being used without enough peace, humility, or self-control.

This chapter is about learning to recognize the drift, respond with wisdom, and repair quickly—so pressure doesn't turn into permanent damage.

## Peter: A Gifted Man in the Middle of Fear

If you want a biblical picture of strength and shadow, Peter is one of the most honest examples in Scripture.

When Peter is healthy, he's bold. He's devoted. He's willing to speak up, step out, try again. He's the one who says, "Lord, if it's you… tell me to come" and then steps out onto the water (Matthew 14:28–29, NIV).

Peter's strength is courage. Initiative. Leadership energy.

But when Peter is under fear, his strength can drift into a shadow. He can become impulsive. Defensive. Overconfident. And at his lowest point, he denies Jesus three times (Luke 22:54–62, NIV).

If you've ever looked back on a moment and thought, "That wasn't me… why did I do that?"—you understand Peter.

Peter's story gives us permission to be honest about a human reality: sometimes we don't lose our values—we lose our composure.

**Strength vs Shadow: The Difference Between Design and Drift**

A strength is a gift God contributes through you. A shadow is what that gift can look like when it's not submitted to love.

Here are a few examples you may recognize:

- Strength: decisiveness → Shadow: control
- Strength: sensitivity → Shadow: people-pleasing
- Strength: confidence → Shadow: arrogance
- Strength: carefulness → Shadow: procrastination
- Strength: optimism → Shadow: denial
- Strength: honesty → Shadow: harshness
- Strength: peacemaking → Shadow: avoidance
- Strength: passion → Shadow: intensity that overwhelms others

The goal is not to eliminate your strength. The goal is to mature it.

Maturity looks like this: the same strength, but with humility. The same gift, but with wisdom. The same wiring, but with love.

## The Most Common Relationship Mistake: Calling Shadow 'Personality'

One of the ways relationships break down is when we label someone's shadow as "just who they are."

"They're just rude."
"They're just lazy."
"They're just dramatic."
"They're just controlling."

Sometimes those labels are describing a pattern. But they're not describing the whole person.

And when we turn a shadow into an identity label, we stop believing growth is possible.

That's why seeing people the way God sees them is so important. God doesn't deny our shadows. But He also doesn't reduce us to them.

## A Coaching Lens: Ask 'Is This Pressure Talking?'

Here's a simple question that will change how you respond in tense moments:

**Is this pressure talking?**

That question does not excuse harmful behavior. It just helps you interpret it correctly.

When pressure is talking, you can do three wise things:

**1) Slow the moment down**

Speed is the enemy of repair. When emotions are hot, clarity is usually low.

**2) Translate the fear underneath**

Shadows often have a fear underneath them:
- control often fears chaos
- avoidance often fears conflict
- harshness often fears being unheard
- people-pleasing often fears rejection

**3) Choose repair over winning**

Winning a moment is easy. Repairing a relationship is mature.

**Try this sentence**

"I think stress is talking right now. Let's pause and come back to this with clarity."

That sentence is not weak. It's wise. It protects the relationship from words you can't take back.

**Repair Is a Spiritual Skill**

If you want your relationships to stay healthy, you have to become good at repair.

Repair is what you do after the shadow shows up. Repair is what you do after the tone was wrong, the timing was wrong, the words were sharp, or the reaction was bigger than the situation.

Jesus didn't teach perfect conflict avoidance. He taught reconciliation.

A simple biblical framework for repair can sound like:

- "I was wrong."
- "I'm sorry."
- "That's not how I want to talk to you."
- "Can we try that again?"

If you can say those sentences, you can keep relationships from breaking over normal human pressure moments.

**Peter's Repair: The Beauty of Being Restored**

Peter's story doesn't end at denial. That's the gospel.

After the resurrection, Jesus restores Peter in a conversation that is both honest and healing (John 21, NIV). Jesus doesn't pretend nothing happened. He asks Peter, "Do you love me?" and then He re-commissions him.

That restoration tells us something powerful: your shadow moment does not have to define your story.

And it also gives us a model: repair is not humiliation. Repair is restoration.

### When You're the One in the Shadow

If you are the one who drifted—if you were sharp, reactive, distant, controlling, passive, or intense—here's what maturity looks like:

**1) Own it quickly**

Don't defend it. Don't explain it away. Own it.

**2) Apologize specifically**

"I'm sorry" is good. "I'm sorry I raised my voice and dismissed you" is better.

**3) Make a small change**

Repair isn't only words. It's a shift—something practical that shows your heart is serious.

### When Someone Else Is in the Shadow

If the other person is the one drifting, seeing them well doesn't mean enabling them. It means you respond to the person without matching the shadow.

Here are three options that keep you in love and wisdom:

- Pause: "Let's take a break and come back."

• Name impact: “That tone lands hard. I want to talk, but not like this.”

• Hold boundary: “I’m willing to keep talking when we can be respectful.”

This is how you protect your peace without becoming cold.

**Memorable moment**

**The goal isn’t perfection. The goal is repair.**

**Optional reflection**

Think about your most common stress drift.
1) What pressure triggers it?
2) What fear might be underneath it?
3) What is one repair sentence you can practice this week?

**Prayer**

Jesus, thank You for Peter's honest story and Your restoring love. Teach me to recognize stress in myself and others without shame. Give me self-control under pressure and humility to repair quickly. Help me mature the strengths You've given me, and respond wisely when others are in their shadow. In Your name, amen.

**Bridge to Chapter 6**: Once we recognize strengths and shadows, we can begin learning simple translation lenses—helpful vocabulary that supports God's design rather than replacing it.

# Chapter 6: Translation Lenses — Tools That Help Us Understand Differences (Without Putting People in Boxes)

By now, we've set a foundation that is stronger than any personality tool: what God made is "very good." And when you learn to see people the way God sees them, you stop treating difference like an interruption and start treating it like design.

So why talk about tools like DISC, Myers-Briggs, the Enneagram[3], or even something as simple as Love Languages[4]? Because sometimes you don't need a new belief—you need a new vocabulary.

A translation lens gives you language for patterns you're already experiencing. It helps you stop assuming motives and start understanding what a person might be trying to protect.

But we need to say this clearly up front:

**A tool can describe a tendency. Only God transforms the heart.**

Tools are not identity. Tools are not destiny. Tools are not excuses. And a tool should never become a weapon.

This chapter is exploratory on purpose. People don't like homework (I get it!). So we're going to keep this practical, high-level, and life-coach friendly. You'll leave with language you can use today—without having to memorize a chart.

## The Purpose of a Translation Lens

Healthy tools do four things:

- They reduce personal offense. (You stop thinking, "They're doing this to me.")

- They increase compassion without naivety. (You can understand and still hold boundaries.)

- They improve communication. (You learn to translate instead of accuse.)

- They help teams and families "fit" better. (You stop demanding sameness.)

Unhealthy tool-usage does the opposite: it labels, excuses, divides, and hardens.

## The Danger: When People Use 'Type' as a Crutch

One reason many people dislike personality tools is because they've seen the misuse. Someone takes a test and then tries to live to the label—or uses it as a reason not to grow.

"That's just my personality."
"I'm a ________, so you'll just have to deal with it."

That's not maturity. That's hiding.

God does not reveal patterns so we can excuse them. He reveals patterns so we can steward them.

### A Simple Rule: Use Tools as Mirrors, Not Masks

Here's a life-changing way to keep tools healthy:

**Use tools as mirrors, not masks.**

A mirror helps you see yourself more clearly so you can grow. A mask helps you avoid responsibility while looking "explained."

The moment a tool becomes a mask, it stops serving love.

### Myers-Briggs at a High Level: Everyday Differences That Matter

Let's start simple—because most relationship tension comes from simple differences.

### Lists vs. Spontaneity

Some people feel calmer with a plan, a list, and a decision. Others feel calmer with flexibility, options, and room to adjust.

One person is often protecting follow-through. The other is often protecting adaptability.

Scripture makes room for both: there's wisdom in planning ("The plans of the diligent…" Proverbs 21:5, NIV) and wisdom in surrender ("the Lord establishes their steps," Proverbs 16:9, NIV).

### People-Time vs. Alone-Time

Some people recharge with people. Connection fills their tank. Others recharge in quiet. Solitude restores them.

This isn't about who loves people more. It's about how your inner battery refills.

Even Jesus modeled both—present with people, and also withdrawing to pray (Luke 5:16, NIV). So making room for someone's recharge rhythm isn't rejection. It's respect.

### Details vs. Big Picture

Some people naturally see details first. Some people naturally see patterns and possibilities first.

In conflict, the detail person can feel like the vision person is vague. And the vision person can feel like the detail person is nitpicky.

But usually, both are protecting something good: realism and quality on one side, direction and hope on the other. When those lenses work together, outcomes get better.

**DISC: A Practical Workplace and Relationship Translator**

DISC is popular in workplaces for a reason: it gives a quick way to talk about differences without turning them into moral judgments.

At a high level, you'll often see these emphases:

• D (Drive): protects results, momentum, decisiveness.

• I (Influence): protects connection, morale, persuasion.

• S (Steadiness): protects stability, consistency, peace.

• C (Conscientiousness): protects accuracy, quality, troubleshooting.

The healthiest DISC question isn't "What are you?"—it's "What are you protecting right now?"

This is where teams shift. The sales lens often protects momentum and opportunity. The technician lens often protects quality and feasibility. Instead of calling each other careless or negative, you learn to say, "We need both."

### The Enneagram: Motivation Language (Handle With Care)

The Enneagram is different from DISC and Myers-Briggs in one key way: it often focuses on inner motivation—what drives you, what you fear, what you seek.

That can be useful, because motivation is often what causes conflict. But it's also why the Enneagram needs to be handled with care.

Used well, it increases compassion and self-awareness. Used poorly, it becomes a label that feels permanent—or a shortcut that replaces discipleship and growth.

If you use it, keep it in the "mirror" category. Let it prompt prayer, self-control, and maturity—not excuses.

### Love Languages: A Tool That Helps Without Getting Complicated

Sometimes the simplest tools are the most useful. For many couples and families, learning that people both express and experience love differently is a game-changer.

One person hears "I love you" most clearly through words. Another feels love most clearly through help, time, gifts, or affection.

When you realize, "Oh—we're both loving, we're just speaking different love languages," resentment decreases and connection increases.

### How Scripture Keeps Tools Healthy

Tools are most helpful when they stay under Scripture's call to love and maturity.

Scripture gives us two guardrails:

First, it calls us to humility and teachability—"quick to listen" (James 1:19, NIV). Most relationships improve simply because we stop assuming and start listening.

Second, it calls us to build up rather than tear down—words that strengthen, not words that wound (Ephesians 4:29, NIV). A tool should increase your ability to build people up, not label them down.

### Memorable Moments: Keep These in Your Pocket

**Tools are vocabulary, not verdicts.**

**Labels are easy. Love is skilled.**

**If it makes you feel superior, it's not helping you. If it makes you humble, it can help you grow.**

**Try this sentence**

"Before I assume, let me translate: what are you trying to protect right now?"

OR:

"Help me understand how you got there."

### A Quick Self-Check: When a Tool Is Helping vs. Hurting

A tool is helping when it produces more:

- patience
- understanding
- honor language
- clear boundaries
- better teamwork

A tool is hurting when it produces more:

- superiority
- excuses
- sarcasm or contempt
- stereotyping
- division

**Optional reflection**

Think of one relationship that feels stuck.
1) What difference keeps showing up?
2) What might that difference be protecting?
3) What one sentence could you use this week to translate instead of accuse?

**Prayer**

Father, thank You for the creativity of Your design. Give me wisdom to use tools as mirrors, not masks—vocabulary, not verdicts. Keep my heart humble, my words life-giving, and my relationships full of honor. Teach me to recognize Your workmanship in others and to work with it, not against it. In Jesus' name, amen.

Bridge to Chapter 7: Now that we have translation language, we're going to apply it to real life—starting with family dynamics and parenting lenses.

# Chapter 7: Parenting — Two Good Hearts, Two Different Lenses

Parenting has a way of revealing our wiring fast. Under pressure, we default to what feels loving to us. And when two parents love through different lenses, it can create conflict—or it can create coverage.

If you've ever looked back and wished you could do something differently, you're not alone. Most parents don't need more shame. They need more language, more grace, and better tools for repair.

In Chapter 6 we talked about translation lenses—ways to understand how people are wired without putting them in boxes. This chapter is where we put that into the living room and the kitchen, right where real life happens.

## Two Parenting Styles, One Shared Love

In our home, we had two very different parenting instincts.

My natural style leaned more passive. My internal logic was often, "Why say no if yes will do?" I didn't like unnecessary conflict. I wanted to keep the atmosphere peaceful, and I believed warmth would do the heavy lifting.

My husband leaned more authoritatively. He valued structure, follow-through, and boundaries. Her internal logic was often, “If we don’t lead with clarity, we’re not loving our kids well.”

And here’s the truth: both of those instincts can be beautiful. Warmth matters. Structure matters. Peace matters. Boundaries matter.

But when we didn’t know how to honor each other’s wiring, those strengths collided.

### When Strengths Collide, Kids Feel It First

One of the hardest parts of parenting is realizing that when adults clash, children absorb the atmosphere.

We had our share of great explosions. Different lenses. Different strategies. Different triggers. And if I could go back, I would tell my younger self this:

**Your kids don’t need perfect parents. They need repairing parents.**

Because kids learn more from watching adults repair than they do from watching adults pretend.

I’ll never forget one day when Dubby and I were fighting in the kitchen. It wasn’t quiet. It wasn’t gentle. It was tense. And our oldest daughter was close by.

I noticed she was doing something with her eyes closed, and I asked her what she was doing.

She said, “I’m praying that you and Daddy will stop fighting.”

That is a gut punch. There’s no way around it. When your child starts praying for peace because your home feels unstable, it wakes you up at a soul level.

Dubby and I aimed to be mature enough to appreciate how each of us was wired and then bring the best of both strengths to our children. There were times we succeeded. But life gets loud and under pressure, we often fought against each other’s design instead of teaming up.

**What We Wish We Would Have Done: Turned Differences Into Coverage**

Here is what I wish we would have done, and what I want to coach you toward:

**Don’t compete. Complement.**

A passive-leaning parent often contributes gentleness, empathy, and emotional safety. An authoritative-leaning parent often contributes stability, clarity, and consistent boundaries.

When you blend those strengths, kids get a gift: a home where love is warm and leadership is clear.

When you fight those strengths, kids get mixed messages: one parent becomes the "fun one," the other becomes the "strict one," and the home becomes a tug-of-war.

**The Coaching Shift: Build a Joint Strategy**

One of the most practical leadership moves you can make as parents is to build a joint strategy.

A joint strategy doesn't mean you parent the same way. It means you agree on:

- what matters most
- what your non-negotiables are
- how you will repair when you disagree
- how you will present unity to your children

You can disagree privately, refine your plan, and then come back with a united front. Not because you're pretending—but because your children shouldn't carry adult conflict.

**Try this sentence**

"We're on the same team. Help me understand what you're trying to protect for our kids."

That one sentence instantly changes the tone. It stops the conversation from being "me vs you" and returns it to "us."

### A Simple Parenting Translation Chart

Here are a few common clashes—and the translation that can help:

**If your spouse says: "They need consequences."**

Translation: "I'm trying to protect responsibility and character."

**If your spouse says: "They're just a kid."**

Translation: "I'm trying to protect emotional safety and connection."

**If your spouse says: "You're too hard on them."**

Translation: "I'm afraid we'll damage their heart or break relationship."

**If your spouse says: "You're too easy on them."**

Translation: "I'm afraid we're training entitlement instead of maturity."

When you translate, you stop fighting each other's intent and start building a strategy that holds both sides.

### Repair in Front of Your Kids (Yes, Sometimes)

Kids don't need to witness everything. But they do need to witness repair.

A simple repair in front of your kids can sound like:

- "Mom and Dad were frustrated, and we spoke sharply. That's not okay."

- "We love each other, and we're going to talk respectfully."

- "We're working it out, and you are safe."

Those sentences create stability. They teach kids that conflict isn't catastrophe and that love knows how to come back together.

**When You're Co-Parenting and You're Not Aligned**

Some readers will be in situations where parenting alignment isn't easy—maybe you're co-parenting after divorce, or you're parenting with a spouse who won't engage in joint strategy.

If that's you, here's a compassionate truth: you can't control the other parent's choices, but you can control the culture you create in your home.

You can become the parent who is consistent, safe, and clear. You can model repair. You can model honor. And you can refuse to speak contempt into your child's heart about the other parent.

That matters more than you think.

**Memorable moment**

**A peaceful home isn't built by avoiding conflict. It's built by learning repair.**

**Optional reflection**

If you're parenting with another adult, ask:
1) What is my natural parenting lens?
2) What is theirs?
3) What strength does each of us bring?
4) What is one joint strategy conversation we need to have this month?

**Prayer**

Father, thank You for children and the sacred stewardship of shaping hearts. Give me humility to learn, courage to repair, and wisdom to build a healthy home culture. Teach me to honor the other parent's strengths, to translate differences, and to lead with love and clarity. Heal what's been wounded in our family story, and help us become the safest people for our children. In Jesus' name, amen.

**Bridge to Chapter 8**: Parenting is one of the clearest places differences collide. Another is the workplace—where different strengths have to work together to serve customers, solve problems, and build a healthy culture.

# Chapter 8: Workplace — Don't Hire Mirrors, Hire Supply

If parenting is where differences collide at home, the workplace is where differences collide under pressure—deadlines, customers, quality expectations, money, and stress.

Workplaces are one of the fastest places to discover something true: you cannot build anything meaningful with mirrors.

A mirror is someone just like you—same lens, same strengths, same preferences. Mirrors feel easy. Mirrors feel smooth. But mirrors don't build strong teams.

Supply builds strong teams.

Supply is what someone else brings that you don't naturally carry. It's the gift that covers your blind spot. It's the strength that complements your weakness.

**If we want healthy workplaces, we have to learn to value supply.**

And this is exactly where understanding design differences becomes practical, because toxic work environments often begin with one simple thing: we stop interpreting differences as supply and start interpreting them as opposition.

### The Two Lenses That Often Clash: Broad Stroke and Fine Detail

Let me give you a real-life example that played out repeatedly in our businesses.

In the workplace, we had different kinds of people doing different kinds of work. Some were naturally sales-oriented. They could see opportunity fast. They could communicate confidently. They could cast a vision for a project. They were often willing to take action with incomplete information because momentum mattered.

Others were technicians—highly analytical, troubleshooting oriented, detail-aware. They could see what could go wrong. They could spot the missing pieces. They were often the people who saved us from expensive mistakes.

If you've ever been in an organization, you know this tension: the broad-stroke people think the detail people are slowing everything down. The detail people think the broad-stroke people are careless.

Both sides are usually protecting something good. Sales often protects momentum and opportunity. Technicians often protect quality and feasibility.

When those two sides don't respect each other, the environment becomes "us vs them."

## How 'Us vs Them' Starts

"Us vs them" usually begins with these small, familiar sentences:

- "They never think about the details."
- "They always get in the weeds."
- "They don't understand how business works."
- "They don't care about quality."
- "They don't care about getting the job."

Those sentences feel like facts when you're frustrated. But most of the time they're not facts—they're interpretations.

And when we interpret differences as disrespect, we build walls.

## A Tool That Helped Us Translate: DISC (Used as a Lens, Not a Label)

In our work environment, DISC was one of the most helpful translation tools we used, because it gave us language that lowered offense.

Generally speaking, the people with strong analytical, troubleshooting gifts often scored high in the "C"

(Conscientiousness) lane—they cared about accuracy, quality, and getting it right.

And the people who were more naturally driven, action-oriented, and comfortable with broad strokes were often in the D/I blend—they could make quick decisions, build relationships, and move things forward.

Used well, DISC helped us stop personalizing differences. Instead of calling each other careless or negative, we learned to say, "We're seeing this from different lenses."

### The Estimating and Quoting Problem: Why Both Lenses Matter

One of the biggest practical flashpoints was estimating and quoting.

On the quoting side, you often have to work in broad strokes. You need enough detail to be responsible, but you cannot spend more time quoting a job than doing the job. That's not good stewardship, and it's not good business.

On the technician side, when the actual work begins, the details matter. Technicians can see the missing pieces and the potential failures—and that input is gold.

So the problem wasn't that one side was right and the other was wrong. The problem was that we needed a workflow that honored both lenses.

**The Coaching Shift: Build a Translation Workflow**

Here are a few practical ways we learned to translate differences into a healthier culture:

**1) Invite the technician voice early—on purpose**

Instead of waiting until the last minute to hear what could go wrong, include technical thinkers early in the brainstorming stage. They'll save you time, money, and embarrassment.

**2) Set clear expectations for "good enough"**

Perfection is not always possible. Part of leadership is deciding what level of detail is needed at each stage. When you name that clearly, the detail people feel respected—and the momentum people can move forward without shame.

**3) Separate 'idea time' from 'execution time'**

In idea time, you want a wide net—vision, possibility, problem-spotting, what-if thinking. In execution time, you want decisions, timelines, and follow-through. If you mix those two stages, meetings turn into frustration.

**4) Honor language changes the air**

Teams become toxic when people feel unseen. Honor doesn't remove accountability—it removes contempt.

**Try this sentence**

"We need both lenses. What are you seeing that I might be missing?"

That one sentence can stop "us vs them" in its tracks, because it turns difference into supply.

## A Word for Leaders: Your Job Is Culture

If you lead people—whether you own a company, manage a team, or lead a department—your job is not just results. Your job is culture.

Culture is the air people breathe. It's the emotional climate. It's what feels normal.

A healthy culture doesn't pretend everyone is the same. A healthy culture creates a place where different strengths can contribute without being mocked, minimized, or weaponized.

Scripture reminds us that different parts of the body matter (see 1 Corinthians 12, NIV). Workplaces thrive when we stop asking, "Why aren't they like me?" and start asking, "What supply did God place in them for this team?"

**Memorable moment**

**A healthy team doesn't erase differences. It translates them into strength.**

**Optional reflection**

Think about your current workplace (or the last one you were in).
1) Where do you see an "us vs them" pattern?
2) What difference is being interpreted as opposition instead of supply?
3) What is one sentence you could use this week to bring honor into the air?

**Prayer**

Father, thank You for the variety of gifts You place in teams. Teach me to value supply instead of demanding mirrors. Give me wisdom to translate differences, humility to listen, and courage to build healthy culture where people can do their best work. Help me represent You well in the workplace. In Jesus' name, amen.

**Bridge to Chapter 9**: Once you start translating differences, you can begin cleaning up toxic environments—especially the "us vs them" culture that divides teams and drains people.

# Chapter 9: Cleaning Up Toxic Workplaces by Breaking the Us vs Them Mentality

If you've ever walked into a workplace and felt the air—heavy, sharp, divided—you already know: toxicity is rarely one big moment. It's usually a pattern that becomes normal.

And one of the fastest ways toxicity grows is when a team slips into an "us vs them" mindset.

This chapter is not about blaming industries, bosses, or coworkers. It's about giving you a practical, hope-filled way to shift the culture—whether you're the owner, the manager, the team lead, or the employee who wants to represent God well where you work.

Because the workplace is one of the main places we spend our lives. If we can learn to see people the way God sees them at work, we can change the atmosphere in a way that impacts customers, families, and communities.

## First, Let's Define 'Toxic' (Without Getting Weird About It)

When people say a workplace is toxic, they usually don't mean "We have hard days." They mean something deeper—an emotional environment where stress is constant, respect is scarce, and relationships are unsafe.

Toxic patterns can include:

- sarcasm as a normal language
- contempt and eye-rolling
- gossip as entertainment
- constant blame and scapegoating
- unclear expectations with constant criticism
- "favorites" and unfair standards
- people walking on eggshells

And here's what makes toxicity so exhausting: it doesn't just affect performance. It affects people's bodies. When the air is unsafe, people stay in survival mode.

**The Bible Gives Us a Culture Shift: We're Builders, Not Destroyers**

Scripture has a simple cultural principle that applies anywhere people work together: use your words to build, not to tear down.

Paul says our words should build people up "according to their needs" so they give grace to those who hear (Ephesians 4:29, NIV). That's not church talk—that's culture talk.

A toxic workplace is often a workplace where words stop giving grace.

### How 'Us vs Them' Gets Born

An "us vs them" mindset usually starts innocently. It often begins with real differences—departments, roles, personalities, and responsibilities.

Sales sees the world one way. Operations sees it another way. Management sees pressures employees may not see. Employees see realities management may not see.

The problem isn't the differences. The problem is the interpretation.

When differences are interpreted as disrespect, we build camps. We start telling stories about the other side. And the story becomes more powerful than the truth.

### The Coaching Shift: Translate Differences into Supply

In Chapter 8 we talked about mirrors vs supply. That idea is a culture-changer:

**Supply is not opposition. Supply is coverage.**

When you shift from "they're the problem" to "they may be covering a blind spot," you begin breaking toxicity at the root.

**A Practical Map: What Each Side Often Protects**

Here's a quick translation map you can use when tension rises between groups:

• Sales often protects momentum, opportunity, and relationships.

• Operations often protects feasibility, capacity, and follow-through.

• Technicians often protect quality, safety, and accuracy.

• Admin often protects order, clarity, and compliance.

• Leadership often protects sustainability, stewardship, and long-term mission.

This is not a stereotype chart. It's a translation tool. It helps you ask the right question: "What are they trying to protect?"

## Four Culture Moves That Clean Up Toxicity

### 1) Stop sideways talk

Gossip feels like relief, but it's actually a slow poison. If you want culture to change, bring problems to the right person, not the wrong people.

A simple guideline is: if you wouldn't say it with them in the room, it probably doesn't belong in your mouth.

### 2) Create clarity, then create consistency

Toxicity grows in confusion. Clear expectations and consistent standards reduce anxiety.

If you lead people, clarity is kindness. If you don't lead people, asking for clarity is maturity.

### 3) Build honor language into your normal

Honor language changes the air. It doesn't remove accountability—it removes contempt.

Honor can sound like:
- "Thank you for catching that."
- "I appreciate how thorough you are."
- "That perspective helps us."
- "I can see what you're protecting."

### 4) Repair quickly (don't let resentment set up shop)

Resentment is what happens when repair gets delayed. Most people don't need a perfect workplace—they need a workplace where issues are addressed and relationships are treated with dignity.

**Try this sentence**

"Help me understand what you're protecting—and what you need from us to do this well."

If you're a leader, you can also use:

"I want us to win together. What's one change that would make this healthier?"

## When You're Not the Boss: What You Can Still Do

You may be thinking, "This is great, but I'm not in charge." Even if you're not in charge, you still have influence.

Here are a few influence moves that don't require a title:

- Refuse contempt. Don't join the eye-roll culture.
- Ask translation questions instead of making accusations.
- Name the good you see in people's intent.
- Bring solutions, not just complaints.

One healthy person can shift a room. Not by being preachy—by being steady, honorable, and wise.

### When You're the Leader: Culture Is Your Job

If you lead people, your job is not only results. Your job is culture.

Culture is the air. It's what feels normal. And if you want culture to change, you have to reward the culture you want.

Reward honor. Reward repair. Reward clarity. Reward collaboration. Don't reward gossip, sarcasm, or blame—even if the person doing it is talented.

Talent without character is expensive.

**Memorable moment**

**Toxicity isn't only a work problem. It's an honor problem.**

**Optional reflection**

Think of your workplace environment.
1) Where do you see an "us vs them" mindset?
2) What might the other side be trying to protect?
3) What is one sentence you can use this week to bring honor into the air?

**Prayer**

Father, help me represent You well at work. Deliver me from gossip, contempt, and hidden superiority. Give me wisdom to translate differences and courage to speak with honor. Help me be a builder—someone whose words give grace and whose presence brings peace. In Jesus' name, amen.

**Bridge to Chapter 10**: Once the "us vs them" mentality starts breaking, the next skill is clean conflict—how to address real issues without losing love, dignity, or unity.

# Chapter 10: Clean Conflict and Quick Repair — How to Address Issues Without Losing Love

By now we've built some key muscles: starting from "very good," seeing people well, protecting unity, recognizing strength and shadow, translating differences, and cleaning up "us vs them" culture.

Now we need one more essential skill if we want real-world relationships to thrive: learning how to handle conflict without losing love.

Because conflict isn't proof that people are bad. Conflict is proof that people are human. The real question is not whether conflict shows up. The question is what we do with it when it does.

Healthy communities aren't the ones with no conflict. They're the ones with clean conflict and quick repair.

**Clean conflict is truth with dignity. Quick repair is humility without drama.**

## Acts 6: A Real Complaint Handled With Wisdom

If you want a biblical picture of clean conflict, Acts 6 is one of the best.

A complaint arose in the early church because some widows were being overlooked in the daily distribution of food (Acts 6:1, NIV). That's not a small issue. Food distribution is survival. Overlooking widows is serious.

What I love is that the leaders didn't pretend it wasn't happening. They also didn't shame the people for bringing the complaint.

They named the issue, gathered the community, and created a solution. They appointed people to handle the distribution so it would be fair and consistent (Acts 6:2–4, NIV).

Notice the pattern:

- the issue was named
- the right people were involved
- a practical solution was built
- unity was protected
- the mission moved forward

That is clean conflict.

**The Two Ditches: Avoidance and Explosion**

Most people fall into one of two ditches when conflict shows up.

**Ditch #1: Avoidance**

Avoidance says, "If I don't talk about it, it will go away."

But unspoken conflict doesn't disappear. It usually turns into resentment.

**Ditch #2: Explosion**

Explosion says, "I'm going to say it all, say it now, and say it loud."

Explosion can feel honest, but it often damages trust. It can turn a solvable problem into a relationship wound.

Clean conflict is the middle path: honest, respectful, and solution-minded.

**A Coaching Framework: Heat, Truth, and Love**

When conflict gets messy, it's usually because we have one of these three out of balance:

- Heat (emotion) is high
- Truth (clarity) is unclear
- Love (honor) is leaking

A clean conflict conversation doesn't eliminate emotion. It reduces unnecessary heat, increases clarity, and protects honor.

## Jesus' Simple Path: Go to the Person First

Jesus gave a practical relational principle: go to the person first (see Matthew 18:15, NIV).

That is not always easy. But it prevents sideways talk. It protects relationships from gossip, triangulation, and story-making.

A clean conflict question is: "Am I talking to the right person?"

### Try this sentence

"I want to understand and resolve this—not win against you. Can we talk?"

That sentence sets the tone. It tells the other person, "I'm not here to attack. I'm here to repair."

## How to Have a Clean Conflict Conversation

### Step 1: Start with honor

Honor doesn't mean agreement. Honor means dignity. Start by naming the good you see.

Examples:

- "I know you care about this."
- "I appreciate your effort."
- "I can see you're carrying a lot."

**Step 2: Name the issue clearly (no villain language)**

Instead of, "You always…" or "You never…," name the specific behavior and the impact.

Examples:

- "When the deadline changes last minute, I feel anxious and unprepared."

- "When the tone gets sharp, I shut down and it's hard for me to stay engaged."

- "When decisions get made without input, I feel dismissed."

**Step 3: Ask a translation question**

This keeps you out of assumption and invites understanding.

Examples:

- "Help me understand what you were protecting in that moment."

- "What matters most to you about this?"

- "What were you hoping would happen?"

**Step 4: Make a clear request**

Requests are healthier than complaints. Be specific.

Examples:

- "Could we decide deadlines 24 hours earlier?"
- "Can we pause when the tone rises and restart respectfully?"
- "Can we agree on one decision-maker for this project?"

**Step 5: Build a next step**

End with action—not just emotion.

Examples:

- "Let's try this for two weeks and revisit."
- "Let's write down our process so we're consistent."
- "Let's check in Friday and see what improved."

**Quick Repair: The 'Reset' Skill**

Even with the best tools, you'll still have moments where the shadow shows up. That's why repair is everything.

A quick repair doesn't require a long speech. It requires humility.

Here are a few "reset" sentences that save relationships:

- "That came out wrong. Let me try again."
- "I'm sorry. I was defensive."
- "I care about you. I don't want to talk like that."
- "Can we reset?"

If you can learn to reset quickly, you'll prevent little conflicts from becoming big wounds.

**When It's Not Safe to Have the Conversation**

There are situations where a direct conversation is not wise or safe—especially if someone is consistently abusive, manipulative, or unwilling to be respectful.

In those situations, clean conflict may look like strong boundaries, documentation, or involving appropriate support. Honor doesn't require you to stay in harm.

But for most everyday conflicts—family, friendships, workplaces—clean conflict is one of the most loving skills you can develop.

**Memorable moment**

**The goal isn't to avoid conflict. The goal is to keep love clean while you solve real problems.**

**Optional reflection**

Think of one conflict you've been avoiding.
1) What is the real issue?
2) What is the 'good' you can name before you address it?
3) What is one clear request you can make?
4) What reset sentence do you want ready when emotions rise?

**Prayer**

Father, teach me to handle conflict with maturity. Deliver me from gossip, avoidance, and contempt. Give me courage to speak, humility to listen, and wisdom to build solutions. Help me repair quickly when I'm wrong and respond with honor when others are stressed. Make me a peacemaker who tells the truth with love. In Jesus' name, amen.

**Bridge to Chapter 11:** Once you learn clean conflict and quick repair, the next step is learning truth without heat—how to help people grow with honor, the way Scripture models.

# Chapter 11: Truth Without Heat — How to Help People Grow with Honor

If Chapter 10 was about clean conflict, Chapter 11 is about something just as practical: how to tell the truth in a way that doesn't scorch the relationship.

Because if we're going to learn to live with people—families, friendships, teams, communities—we're going to need a skill that many of us were never taught:

**Correction without humiliation.**

We've all seen the opposite. Truth delivered with heat. Feedback delivered with sarcasm. "Help" delivered as a power move.

And let's be honest—sometimes the reason people avoid spiritual conversations, workplace conversations, or even family conversations is not because they hate truth. It's because they've been wounded by the way truth was delivered.

So let's learn the Jesus way: truth with dignity. Clarity with kindness. Courage with humility.

## Priscilla and Aquila: A Quiet Masterclass in Honor

Acts 18 gives us one of my favorite "how to help someone grow" moments in Scripture.

There's a man named Apollos. The Bible describes him as "learned" and "competent," and he speaks with passion (Acts 18:24–25, NIV).

In other words, he's gifted. He's sincere. He's not trying to mislead anyone. He's doing the best he can with what he knows.

But Priscilla and Aquila—two mature believers—recognize something: Apollos needs fuller understanding. So what do they do?

They don't correct him publicly. They don't embarrass him. They don't start a debate to prove who's smarter. They take him aside and explain "the way of God more adequately" (Acts 18:26, NIV).

That is truth without heat.

And it's powerful because it shows us a principle we can use in every setting—not only spiritual settings: when someone is trying, gifted, and sincere, honor is the doorway to growth.

## Why Heat Breaks People (Even When You're Right)

Heat is what happens when truth is mixed with contempt, impatience, superiority, or frustration.

Heat can show up as:

- sarcasm
- public embarrassment
- labels ("You always…" "You never…")
- tone that says, "How could you not know this?"

Even if the content is accurate, heat often triggers defensiveness. And once someone is defending their dignity, they can't hear your wisdom.

This is why Scripture values gentleness. Gentleness is not weakness—it's strength under control.

Honor Is Not Flattery. Honor Is Accuracy.

Some people worry that honor means we can't be honest. Not true.

Honor is not pretending. Honor is accuracy about God's workmanship in a person.

Priscilla and Aquila didn't ignore what was missing in Apollos. They simply addressed it in a way that protected his dignity.

That's what we're after: truth that builds, not truth that bruises.

A Coaching Framework: The 4 P's of Truth Without Heat

Here's a simple framework you can use anywhere—marriage, parenting, friendships, workplace leadership.

1) Permission

Before you correct, ask permission. It lowers defenses and communicates respect.

Example: "Can I share an observation that might help?"

2) Private

Correct privately whenever possible. Public correction often becomes public shame.

Priscilla and Aquila "took him aside." That phrase carries wisdom.

3) Positive intent

Name the good you see first. Not as manipulation—because it's true.

Example: "I can see you care about doing this well. That's one of your strengths."

4) Practical next step

Don't just critique. Give a next step. Growth needs a handle.

Example: "Next time, can we try ___?" or "Here's one adjustment that would strengthen this."

Try this sentence

"I can see the gift on you. Can I offer one thought that might strengthen it?"

If the setting is work or family and you want a non-spiritual translation, try:

"I see what you're going for. Can I share one adjustment that would make it even stronger?"

How to Receive Correction Without Losing Yourself

Now let's talk about the other side—because if we want healthy community, we have to learn to receive truth well.

Receiving correction is hard, especially if you've been criticized, shamed, or misunderstood in your past.

But here's a mature reframe:

**Correction is not always rejection.**

Sometimes correction is investment.

Proverbs says, "Wounds from a friend can be trusted" (Proverbs 27:6, NIV). Not because wounds are fun, but because a wise friend cares enough to tell the truth.

A quick receiving tool: Pause, Parse, Pray

• Pause: Don't defend immediately.

• Parse: Ask, "Is there a piece of truth I can take?"

• Pray: "God, show me what You want me to learn here."

You don't have to accept every opinion. But you can stay teachable without becoming crushed.

When Someone Uses Heat: How to Stay Clear

Sometimes people don't bring truth with honor. They bring truth with heat.

When that happens, you still have options that keep you strong and kind:

• Name it: "I want to hear you, but the tone is landing harsh."

• Pause it: "Let's take a break and come back."

• Redirect it: "Can you tell me the specific change you're asking for?"

**Optional reflection**

Think of one person you want to help grow (or one relationship where you need to speak truth).

1) What is the 'good' you can name accurately?
2) What is the one clear truth that needs to be said?
3) What is the practical next step you can offer?
4) What sentence will you use to keep it free of heat?

**Prayer**

Father, make my words life-giving. Teach me truth without heat—clarity without cruelty. Give me humility to correct with honor and courage to receive correction with wisdom. Help me be like Priscilla and Aquila—safe, truthful, and constructive. In Jesus' name, amen.

**Bridge to Chapter 12**: Sometimes growth requires a conversation. And sometimes wisdom requires a change of lanes. Next we'll talk about the kind of separation Scripture treats as wisdom—not rejection—and how to walk it out without bitterness.

# Chapter 12: When Separate Paths Are Wisdom — A Holy Skill for Healthy People

We've talked about unity, translation, clean conflict, and truth without heat. So you might assume the next step is simple: stay together, work it out, and never separate.

But Scripture is more honest—and more practical—than that.

Sometimes the most loving thing you can do is stop forcing a fit that keeps draining everyone involved.

That doesn't mean you stop loving. It doesn't mean you become bitter. It doesn't mean you're quitting on people.

**It means you're learning a holy skill: discernment.**

And yes, discernment is a spiritual word—because it's a spiritual practice. But it's also a deeply practical life skill.

Acts 15: Paul and Barnabas — A Separation Without a Villain

Acts 15 tells a story that surprises many readers, because it doesn't fit the "perfect community" idea people sometimes attach to the Bible.

Paul and Barnabas—two leaders who had served together—had a sharp disagreement about whether to take John Mark on their next journey (Acts 15:36–40, NIV).

Luke doesn't sanitize the moment. He says the disagreement "became so sharp" that they parted company (Acts 15:39, NIV).

And here's what's important for our conversation: Scripture doesn't create a villain.

It doesn't say, "Paul was right and Barnabas was wrong," or the other way around. It simply tells us what happened: they separated, and the mission continued.

Sometimes separation is not rejection. Sometimes it's a re-routing so everyone can keep moving forward in health.

Why This Chapter Matters: Many People Carry Shame About 'Not Making It Work'

In real life, people carry a lot of shame around separation.

They think:
• "If I were more loving, I could make this work."
• "If I were more mature, we would never need distance."
• "If I walk away, I'm failing."

Sometimes those thoughts are rooted in devotion. Sometimes they're rooted in fear. And sometimes they're rooted in a misunderstanding of what God asks from us.

God calls us to love. He calls us to honor. He calls us to pursue peace. But He does not call us to force every relationship into the same shape.

A Simple Lens: Fit vs. Value

Here's a coaching distinction that will save you years of confusion:

**You can value someone deeply without being the best fit to partner closely.**

Fit is about alignment of roles, rhythms, communication style, and assignment. Value is about dignity, honor, and love.

When people confuse fit with value, they stay in situations that drain them and call it faithfulness.

Sometimes faithfulness looks like staying. And sometimes faithfulness looks like shifting lanes so both people can thrive.

The first pastor I served under had a leadership style that aligned with mine. We were a great fit. I'm the kind of person who needs some flexibility. On Myers-Briggs language, I'm a strong "P"—I tend to do my best work when I can honor my natural rhythms, listen for what God is doing, and move with that.

But when that pastor left and a new pastor came in, his leadership style was much more structured. He needed me to be much more structured too.

We tried to make it work for several years. But the experience was not life-giving. And the hardest part is I didn't recognize it as a "fit" issue.

So we kept pushing. We kept trying. We kept forcing the shape.

As a result, we had what I would call my biggest failure in ministry.

And then God spoke something that changed my understanding: "I have to separate your ministries for the health of both ministries."

I had to resign, and it was hard. I had been there from the ground up. We had built a new church building. I had been part of holding things together in the transition.

And when I left, I wrestled with the feeling that God had chosen him over me.

Over time, God healed my understanding. It wasn't God choosing one person over another. It was God refusing to let an unhealthy fit destroy both people.

That season was a dark night of the soul. But it also became a doorway. It's what pushed me toward seminary to retool. And later, it positioned me and my husband to start a church that allowed me to work authentically from who God created me to be.

Additionally the pastor was able to clarify his vision and accomplish great things for God.

**How to Separate with Wisdom (Not Bitterness)**

Separation becomes toxic when it is fueled by contempt. Separation becomes wise when it is fueled by stewardship.

1) Name what you can honor

If you can, honor what was good. Honor what the person contributed. Honor what you learned.

2) Be clear about the role shift

Sometimes the relationship doesn't end—it changes shape. A close partnership might become a friendly connection. A daily environment might become a seasonal one.

3) Keep your language clean

Don't rewrite history to justify your pain. Don't recruit people into your bitterness.

4) Let God lead the timeline

Sometimes you separate quickly. Sometimes it's gradual. Sometimes it's a clear decision. But if God is leading, peace will begin to grow.

Try this sentence

"I can honor what we built, and I also recognize this is no longer a healthy fit for me."

If you need a shorter one:

"This season is shifting, and I'm going to follow peace."

Memorable moment

**Separation is not always rejection. Sometimes it's stewardship.**

**Optional Reflection**

Think of one relationship or environment that drains you.
1) Is the issue conflict that needs repair—or fit that needs a lane change?
2) What would a healthy role shift look like?
3) What sentence could you use that honors value while naming fit?

### Prayer

Father, give me wisdom to know when to stay, when to speak, and when to change lanes. Deliver me from guilt that keeps me stuck and bitterness that keeps me bound. Teach me to honor people and honor Your leading. Help me walk in peace, courage, and clean love. In Jesus' name, amen.

**Bridge to Chapter 13**: Once we learn that separation can be wisdom, the next step is learning boundaries without bitterness—how to protect what God is building in you while staying kind and honoring others.

# Chapter 13: Boundaries Without Bitterness — Protecting Peace While Staying Kind

Chapter 12 introduced a truth that can feel both freeing and scary: sometimes separate paths are wisdom.

But even when separation isn't the answer, boundaries often are.

Boundaries are one of the most misunderstood relationship tools—especially for people who love God, love people, and want to live with an open heart.

Some people hear the word boundary and think "wall." Others hear it and think "selfish." But healthy boundaries are neither walls of hate nor acts of selfishness.

**Healthy boundaries are fences of love.**

A fence doesn't exist because you hate your neighbor. A fence exists because you're stewarding what you've been given. It protects what's inside and clarifies what is—and isn't—yours to carry.

This chapter is about learning how to set boundaries without bitterness—how to stay clear without being cold, and how to stay kind without staying stuck.

## Nehemiah: Focused Leadership and Clean 'No'

Nehemiah gives us one of the clearest biblical pictures of boundaries without bitterness.

Nehemiah is rebuilding the wall of Jerusalem. It's a big assignment. It's time-sensitive. It requires focus, teamwork, and courage.

Opposition shows up. And sometimes opposition doesn't look like attack—it looks like distraction.

People ask Nehemiah to come meet with them. It sounds reasonable. It sounds important. But Nehemiah recognizes something: the meeting isn't the mission.

So he responds with a sentence that is famous for a reason: "I am doing a great work and cannot come down" (Nehemiah 6:3, NIV).

Notice the tone. He isn't insulting. He isn't defensive. He isn't dramatic. He's clear.

That is the heart of boundaries: clarity.

Why Boundaries Feel Hard (Especially for Good People)

Boundaries often feel hard because many of us confuse being loving with being available.

We think:

- "If I say no, I'm not loving."
- "If I disappoint someone, I've failed."
- "If I protect my peace, I'm being selfish."

But love is not the same thing as over-functioning.

Jesus loved people perfectly—and He still didn't meet every demand. He withdrew to pray. He moved on to other towns. He slept in storms. He was not driven by human urgency. He was led by the Father.

That's our model: love led, not love bullied.

### Bitterness vs. Boundaries: How to Tell the Difference

Here's a quick way to tell whether you're setting a boundary or building a wall:

A boundary is motivated by stewardship.

It says, "I want health. I want peace. I want love to remain."

A wall is motivated by contempt or fear.

It says, "I'm done with you. I don't care."

You can set strong boundaries and still keep your heart clean.

### What Boundaries Protect

Boundaries most often protecting one of these:

- your time
- your emotional energy
- your focus
- your family's peace
- your integrity
- your calling and assignment
- your physical health

When you know what you're protecting, saying no becomes less personal and more purposeful.

### The Coaching Shift: Stop Explaining Yourself to Death

One reason boundaries get messy is because we over-explain. Over-explaining is often a sign we're trying to manage someone's feelings instead of stewarding our own clarity.

Nehemiah didn't over-explain. He didn't write a paragraph. He gave a clean sentence.

A clean boundary is usually short, kind, and consistent.

Try this sentence

"I can't carry that right now. I'm protecting what God has asked me to build."

Here are a few other clean boundary sentences you can keep in your pocket:

- "I'm not available for that."
- "That doesn't work for me."
- "I can do X, but I can't do Y."
- "I need to think about that and get back to you."
- "I'm not willing to continue this conversation if the tone stays disrespectful."

**Boundaries in Three Common Places**

1) Boundaries with time

Time boundaries are often the first place peace returns. If your schedule has no margin, everything becomes reactive.

A time boundary might sound like: "I can meet for 30 minutes," or "I'm not available after 7 pm."

2) Boundaries with communication

Some people want constant access. Some want immediate replies. A boundary can clarify expectations without offense.

Example: "I don't take work calls on Sundays," or "I respond to messages during business hours."

3) Boundaries with behavior

This is where people often feel guilty, but it's also where dignity is protected.

A behavior boundary sounds like: "I'm willing to talk when we can be respectful. If we can't, I'm going to step away."

You're not punishing someone. You're protecting peace.

**How to Hold Boundaries Without Becoming Hard**

The danger with boundaries is not that we set them. The danger is that we let them turn into hardness.

Here are three ways to keep your heart soft while your boundary stays strong:

1) Bless people in your heart

You don't have to agree with someone to bless them. If your heart stays bitter, you stay bound—even if you have distance.

2) Don't recruit others into your boundary

A boundary is not a gossip campaign. Keep your language clean. Keep your story simple.

3) Be consistent

Inconsistency creates confusion. If you set a boundary and then break it repeatedly, you train people not to respect it.

Memorable moment

**Clarity is kindness. A clean 'no' can be an act of love.**

**Optional reflection**

Where do you most often say yes out of guilt?
1) What are you trying to protect?
2) What clean sentence could you use instead of over-explaining?
3) What boundary would help you stay loving without becoming resentful?

**Prayer**

Father, teach me boundaries without bitterness. Give me courage to say no cleanly, and humility to stay kind. Help me protect what You've asked me to build, and deliver me from guilt that keeps me overextended. Make my 'yes' strong and my 'no' peaceful. In Jesus' name, amen.

**Bridge to Chapter 14**: Boundaries protect peace, but relationships also require forgiveness. Next we'll talk about the difference between forgiving and trusting—and how to walk in freedom without becoming naïve.

# Chapter 14: Forgiveness and Trust — Freedom Without Naivety

If Chapter 13 was about boundaries, Chapter 14 is about the heart that makes boundaries possible: forgiveness.

Forgiveness is one of the most powerful relationship skills God gives us—and also one of the most misunderstood.

Some people hear forgiveness and think, "So I just pretend it didn't happen?" Others hear forgiveness and think, "So I have to let them back into full access?"

No. Forgiveness is not pretending. And forgiveness is not automatic trust.

**Forgiveness sets you free. Trust is rebuilt.**

This chapter is about living in freedom without becoming naïve—how to forgive with a clean heart while also stewarding wisdom, safety, and boundaries.

## Joseph: Forgiveness With Wisdom

If you want a biblical picture of forgiveness and trust, Joseph's story is one of the clearest.

Joseph was betrayed by his own brothers. They sold him, lied about him, and left him for dead in their hearts (Genesis 37, NIV).

Years later, Joseph rises to a position of leadership in Egypt. And then the day comes when his brothers stand in front of him—needing help, not even recognizing who he is.

Joseph has a choice in that moment: revenge or redemption.

And what we see in Joseph is not a shallow forgiveness. It's a strong forgiveness.

Joseph weeps. Joseph speaks truth. Joseph tests character. Joseph provides. He forgives—but he also watches whether trust can be rebuilt.

That combination is mature: tender heart, wise process.

## The Difference Between Forgiveness and Reconciliation

Let's define these clearly, because a lot of people get trapped right here.

Forgiveness

Forgiveness is what you do in your heart. It means you release your right to revenge. It means you refuse to let bitterness become your identity.

## Reconciliation

Reconciliation is what happens in a relationship when both people are willing. It requires honesty, responsibility, and change.

Forgiveness can be one-sided. Reconciliation cannot.

## Why God Calls Us to Forgive

God's call to forgive is not God minimizing your pain. It's God protecting your freedom.

Bitterness is heavy. It drains your energy. It narrows your heart. It keeps you emotionally tied to the person who hurt you.

Forgiveness is how you cut the cord.

Jesus taught us to pray forgiveness into our everyday life—not because God is casual about sin, but because God is serious about freedom.

## Trust: The Language of Access

Trust is not a feeling. Trust is a measure of access.

If you trust someone, they have access to you—your time, your thoughts, your heart, your plans, your vulnerability.

If someone has broken trust, wisdom adjusts access.

That is not bitterness. That is stewardship.

## Joseph's Pattern: Forgiveness With Testing

When Joseph's brothers return, he doesn't instantly hand them full access. He watches. He listens. He tests. He looks for evidence of change.

That's what wise people do. Forgiveness is immediate in the heart. Trust is rebuilt over time.

In other words: Joseph didn't punish them forever. But he also didn't pretend nothing happened.

### Try this sentence

"I forgive you. And trust will take time to rebuild."

If you need a non-spiritual translation:

"I'm choosing to let this go in my heart. But access will be rebuilt slowly."

## Three Signals That Trust Is Rebuilding

You don't rebuild trust with promises. You rebuild trust with patterns.

**Here are three signs trust is rebuilding:**

1) Ownership

The person takes responsibility without excuses.

2) Change

The behavior actually changes over time, not just for a day.

3) Repair

When they mess up, they repair quickly. They don't blame you for being hurt.

When those patterns show up consistently, trust grows.

What Forgiveness Is Not

Let's make this practical. Forgiveness is not:

- denying what happened
- pretending you weren't hurt
- rushing back into full access
- removing consequences from harmful behavior
- staying in danger

Forgiveness is choosing freedom. And freedom requires truth.

## When You're the One Who Needs Forgiveness

This chapter also applies to you if you are the one who broke trust.

A mature response is not just "I'm sorry." It's:

- ownership
- change
- repair
- patience with the rebuilding process

If someone forgives you but doesn't trust you yet, that doesn't mean forgiveness is fake. It means trust is healing.

Memorable moment

**Forgiveness is not full access. Forgiveness is a clean heart.**

### Optional reflection

Think of one relationship where trust has been damaged.

1) What would forgiveness look like in your heart?
2) What boundary or access change is wise right now?
3) What patterns would you need to see for trust to rebuild?
4) What sentence could you use that is both kind and clear?

**Prayer**

Father, thank You for the freedom You offer through forgiveness. Help me release bitterness and choose a clean heart. Give me wisdom to rebuild trust slowly and safely, without naivety. Teach me to forgive like You forgive—truthful, powerful, and free. In Jesus' name, amen.

**Bridge to the Chapter 15**: Forgiveness and trust are how relationships heal. As we finish this book, we'll pull the whole message together: God created you, God created them, and God created us—and His joy is that we would reflect His image together.

# Chapter 15: God Created Us — Putting It All Together

If you've stayed with me this far, I want to say something that might feel obvious—and also deeply powerful:

**God didn't create you for isolation.**

Yes, He created you with unique design. Yes, He calls you "very good." Yes, He's forming your character, healing what's been wounded, and strengthening your confidence in who He made you to be.

But God also created something bigger than "me."

He created "us."

Not a group of identical people who all think the same way, vote the same way, parent the same way, process the same way, and organize their sock drawer the same way. (Let's be honest—some of us don't even have a sock drawer. We have a sock… pile.)

God created a community where different strengths can reflect His image more fully together than any one person can alone.

That's why Scripture uses the language of "one body" and "many parts" (Romans 12:4–5, NIV). Different parts. One purpose.

## The Big Shift This Book Was Really After

Book 2 wasn't meant to turn you into a personality expert. It was to give you a new lens to understand people.

**Here's the shift:**

**From "Why are they like that?" to "What did God place in them on purpose?"**

When you make that shift, everything changes:

- Your offense decreases.
- Your curiosity increases.
- Your words become more life-giving.
- Your boundaries get cleaner.
- Your relationships get safer.
- Your leadership becomes more effective.
- Your home becomes more peaceful.
- Your work environment becomes less toxic.

Not because people suddenly become perfect. But because you stop interpreting difference as disrespect.

God's Dream Isn't Sameness—It's Love

When Jesus talked about how the world would recognize His followers, He didn't say it would be by flawless agreement.

He said it would be by love—"By this everyone will know…" (John 13:35, NIV).

Love is the skill of honoring someone who is not you.

So the true spiritual work in community is not "How do we all become the same?" The work is, "How do we love like Jesus while we stay uniquely designed?"

**A Practical Picture: Three Questions That Build 'Us'**

If you want a simple way to keep building what God is building, use these three questions in your relationships.

1) What strength is God contributing through you?

This keeps you grateful and responsible. You don't shrink your gift, and you don't weaponize your gift.

2) What strength is God contributing through them?

This keeps you honoring. You stop making people the enemy and start seeing supply.

3) What does love require from both of us right now?

This keeps you practical. Love isn't a feeling only. Love is wisdom in action.

The Design Discovery Declaration (and the Next Step)

In Book 1, you created your Design Discovery Declaration—discovering who God literally designed you to be.

This book has been the next step: discovering how God designed other people—and how your design can fit with theirs in real life.

Here's what I want you to hear clearly:

**Your design is not just for your happiness. Your design is for contribution.**

Ephesians calls us God's "workmanship" (Ephesians 2:10, NIV)—His craft, His poem, His handiwork. And then it says we were created to do good works He prepared for us.

That means your wiring is not random. Your story is not wasted. Your strengths are not accidents.

And the people around you are not random either.

Try this sentence

“God, show me what You’re building between us—not just what You’re building in me.”

That sentence shifts your focus from self-protection to partnership.

Five ‘Us’ Practices That Change the Atmosphere

1) Name the good first

Before you correct, before you debate, before you defend—name the good you see. Honor changes the air.

2) Translate before you label

Ask, “What are you trying to protect?” Translation lowers offense and raises understanding.

3) Repair quickly

The goal isn’t perfection. The goal is repair. A quick reset saves relationships.

4) Hold boundaries without bitterness

Clarity is kindness. A clean “no” can be an act of love.

5) Practice unity without demanding agreement

Unity is not always agreement. Sometimes unity looks like listening, respecting, and staying connected while you navigate difference with wisdom.

A Word of Hope: You Can Start Where You Are

Some of you are reading this and thinking, "I wish I would have known this sooner."

I understand that feeling. But shame is not the teacher you need.

If God is showing you something, it's because He wants to heal, grow, and strengthen what's next—not condemn what's behind.

Start where you are. Use one sentence. Ask one better question. Make one repair. Hold one boundary. Small shifts create new culture over time.

Memorable moment

**God's joy is not just that you become whole. It's that we reflect His image together.**

Optional reflection

1) Who is one person God is inviting you to see differently?
2) What do you think God may have placed in them on purpose?
3) What is one 'us' practice you will commit to this week?
4) What is one sentence you want ready when tension rises?

**Prayer**

Father, thank You for Your creativity. Thank You for designing people with purpose and calling them "very good." Teach me to honor the workmanship in others. Help me be a builder of peace, a speaker of life, and a person who reflects Your love in real relationships. Show me what You're building between us, and give me the courage to participate with joy. In Jesus' name, amen.

**Next Steps:** Book 1 helped us discover our design. Book 2 taught us to honor the design in others. So let us pray for strength and wisdom as we walk together and fulfill what God has assigned.

# Epilogue — A Community That Looks Like Heaven

If you're holding this book in your hands (or scrolling it on a screen), you've already done something brave: you've chosen curiosity over cynicism.

You've chosen to believe that people are not problems to solve. They are souls to honor. They are stories to understand. They are workmanship—God's workmanship.

And if you remember one phrase from this entire book, let it be this:

**God created them… and He does not make junk.**

That sentence is not a romantic idea. It's a relational strategy. Because the moment you believe someone was created on purpose, you stop treating them like an inconvenience.

You may still set boundaries. You may still address conflict. You may still say no. But you won't do it from contempt. You'll do it from honor.

God's Picture of 'Us' Is Bigger Than Our Comfort Zone

One of the most beautiful snapshots in Scripture is a picture of people from every nation, tribe, and language—together—worshiping Jesus (Revelation 7:9, NIV).

That verse isn't only about the future. It's a window into God's heart.

He didn't create one flavor of person. He created a masterpiece of variety.

And if heaven looks like diversity with unity, then growth on earth looks like practicing that same skill.

Not forced agreement. Not fake peace. Real love. Real honor. Real humility. Unity that can hold difference without breaking.

**The Holy Work Is Learning to Delight**

Here's a life-coach truth I've learned over the years: you can't build healthy community through tolerance alone.

Tolerance says, "I'll put up with you."

Honor says, "I see God's workmanship in you."

And delight says, "I'm grateful God put you in the world."

Delight doesn't mean you enjoy every behavior. It means you recognize the gift underneath the difference—especially when you're tempted to label it as annoying.

Delight is the opposite of contempt. And contempt is what destroys homes, friendships, workplaces, and communities.

### A Small Daily Practice That Changes the Atmosphere

If you want a practical way to live this book without turning it into homework, here's a simple daily habit:

**Practice 'one sentence of honor.'**

One sentence. One moment. One person.

It can be as simple as:

- "I appreciate the way you think."
- "Thank you for caring about details."
- "You bring calm into the room."
- "Your courage helps us."
- "Your kindness matters."

Honor language is not flattery. It's accuracy. It names real contribution—and it changes the emotional climate.

Try this sentence

"God, show me the gift in this person that I'm missing."

If you want a version you can say out loud to someone:

"I'm learning to see people better. Can I tell you something I appreciate about you?"

A 7-Day 'Us' Challenge (Simple, Not Heavy)

If you're the kind of person who likes a little structure, here's a gentle 7-day practice. If you're not—smile and skip it. (No guilt allowed.)

Day 1: See

Notice one person you usually misunderstand. Ask: "What might they be trying to protect?"

Day 2: Translate

Ask one curiosity question: "Help me understand your lens."

Day 3: Honor

Give one sentence of honor—out loud.

Day 4: Repair

Make one quick repair: "That came out wrong—let me try again."

Day 5: Boundary

Set one clean boundary without over-explaining.

Day 6: Unity

Practice unity without agreement: “I respect you even if we see this differently.”

Day 7: Delight

Thank God for the variety of His design—especially the kind you don’t naturally prefer.

Seven small steps won’t make life perfect. But they will make you a different kind of person in the room—and that changes more than you think.

A Blessing for the Reader

Before we close, I want to speak a blessing over you. Not because you need one more thing to do—but because you need one more reminder of who you already are in God’s eyes.

May you be rooted in the truth that you are God’s workmanship—created on purpose, with purpose.
May you be healed from the places where being misunderstood made you hide.
May you be delivered from contempt—toward yourself and toward others.
May you become fluent in honor language.
May your boundaries be clean and your heart be soft.
May your relationships become safer, not because people are perfect, but because you’ve learned repair.
May you carry the joy of God’s creativity wherever

you go.
And may the people around you feel more "seen" because you chose to see them the way God sees them.

Prayer

Father, thank You for Your creativity. Thank You for the variety of Your design. Forgive us for the ways we've reduced people to labels, or treated differences like interruptions. Teach us to honor Your workmanship in others. Make us people of clean love—truthful, kind, clear, and humble. Let our homes, friendships, workplaces, and communities reflect Your heart. In Jesus' name, amen.

Looking ahead: If Book 1 was about discovering who God created you to be, and Book 2 was about honoring who God created them to be, then Book 3 is about building what God created us for—community that works. Not perfect community. Real community—full of grace, purpose, and joy.

# Endnotes — Tools and Frameworks

The following endnotes provide source references for the assessment tools and frameworks referenced in this book. Endnote numbers correspond to the first mention of each tool in the manuscript.

1. Marston, W. M. (1928). *Emotions of normal people*. Kegan Paul, Trench, Trübner & Co.
Scullard, M., & Baum, D. (2015). *Everything DiSC manual*. Wiley.

2. Jung, C. G. (1921). *Psychological types*. Rascher Verlag.
Myers, I. B., McCaulley, M. H., Quenk, N. L., & Hammer, A. L. (1998). *MBTI manual: A guide to the development and use of the Myers-Briggs Type Indicator* (3rd ed.). Consulting Psychologists Press.

3. Riso, D. R., & Hudson, R. (1999). *The wisdom of the Enneagram: The complete guide to psychological and spiritual growth for the nine personality types*. Bantam Books.

4. Chapman, G. (1992). *The 5 love languages: How to express heartfelt commitment to your mate*. Northfield Publishing.

5. Fortune, D., & Fortune, K. (2009). *Discover your God-given gifts* (Revised & expanded ed.). Chosen Books.

# About the Author

Cindy H. Carr began her faith journey on December 24, 1984. It didn't begin in a church service or with an altar call, but through a personal invitation from Jesus Christ while she was alone preparing for Christmas Eve. In that quiet moment, a relationship was born—one that transcended theology, tradition, and every expectation of what faith was "supposed" to be.

Over the decades that followed, Cindy immersed herself in theological study and served in both business and her community, yet her unwavering relationship with Jesus Christ has guided every step of her life and leadership. She has learned that love—steady, simple, and sincere—is the foundation strong enough to endure any storm.

In *God Made Them, And He Does Not Make Junk*, Cindy builds on the message of Book 1, *God Made You, and He Does Not Make Junk*, inviting readers to move from self-discovery to relationship discovery. Through Scripture, real-life stories, and practical coaching tools, she helps readers recognize God's creativity in the people around them and practice unity without demanding agreement.

www.ingramcontent.com/pod-product-compliance
Lightning Source LLC
LaVergne TN
LVHW010951110826
845149LV00015B/3301
*9781971192048*